How to Find Your Passion in Life

An Essential Guide to Discovering a Sense of Purpose, Finding Your Calling, and Creating Your Own Happiness

by Oscar Cortese

Table of Contents

Introduction

Do you feel unmotivated and sometimes even dragged down by life? Are you deeply discontent with where you find yourself today? Do you find yourself in situations—academic, professional, or personal—where you seem to keep asking yourself, "Why am I here?" Or do you ever ask yourself "What's my purpose on Earth?"

Fortunately, I'm here to tell you that this type of problem doesn't lie with the universe or the world around you; it stems from within yourself. The reason I said "fortunately" is because this is something that can be easily changed!

Allow me to explain. Did you know that the global attitude concerning professional choices has gone through a complete cycle in the last 70 years? Particularly in the US, the 1950s and 60s were marked by the growth of small businesses — the American dream of the successful entrepreneur, which gave rise to the strong upper middle class that has birthed some of today's largest businesses. This was a period where people didn't just think about their careers in terms of money, but also in terms of life aspirations as an integrated set of choices. This was quickly overshadowed in the next generation due to rising inflation and societal pressure to become the next multi-millionaire, and was defined by duty-bound sensibility when it came to vocational selection.

However, that attitude — as seen among many sour-faced middle-to-upper-class management today — has been turned upon its head by the millennial generation. We have entered the second great age of modern innovation, where enthusiasm and drive have yet again become the pillars of successful careers — and curiosity has returned as the driving force.

Now, I'm not going to ask you if you've ever had a great dream to follow—because if you did or if you followed it, you wouldn't need the help of this guide. But, whether you did or not, allow me to help you find your purpose in life.

So if you're looking for that sense of excitement and burning fire beneath your feet every morning when you wake up, then now is the time to allow me to help you find it. At the very least, by following the principles outlined in this guide, you will never again feel that sense of ill-ease or dissatisfaction which makes you question whether your life is headed in the right direction. So, let's get started!

Chapter 1: Dispelling Any Delusions

Much of the discontent we feel is the result of our naive belief that we know ourselves better than anyone else. The single biggest problem which lands us on paths that take us further and further away from our passions is our absolute and undeniably naive certainty that we know ourselves and our likes/dislikes better than anyone else. But, do we? Beyond our tastes in clothes, entertainment, and foods, which other aspects of our personality do we regularly introspect upon and update with any consistency? When was the last time you sat down and thought about how much you've changed what you feel is attractive in a partner since your first? Have you considered this vital aspect of your personality after every relationship, or have you been going round-and-round down the same dysfunctional spirals?

Even if you're one of the rare ones, and have always tweaked your understanding of your taste in partners each time, have you thought about your favorite skill-sets recently? Or the kind of people you love dealing with on a regular basis, or even the kind of environment you'd like to work in? Or have you stuck to the same "dream" you thought you had in 9th grade, and have been a slave to it like a train on rails?

Many of you reading these words may not even have the illusion of a dream, which may be worrying you, but don't worry since you suffer from the same disease as everyone else—concrete delusions of self-awareness.

Growing up, many of us form images of ourselves along the lines of how we perceive ourselves within the world, our place in it, and the additional feedback we get from others around—and we believe that no one except us understands that image with absolute accuracy and certainty. Want proof? Ever notice how almost every teenager—in some fight with an adult, or argument, at least once in their life—will shout out some variation of "you don't even know me" or "no one understands me", etcetera? Well, when most adults grow up, they're deeply mortified when dwelling upon such events in their past, particularly since it turns out that the parents were dead-on about their behavior all along, and it was the kids who never truly got it. Adults among you will know what I mean by this—or at least will relate to some variation of this. As for any teens among you, then your moment of embarrassed realization will come sooner rather than later, because that's the moment you truly enter adulthood.

So, moving on with my point, while we consider personality traits and states of life which we'd like to see ourselves fit in during our daydreams—we think of vocational aspects in terms of professions and jobs and not skill sets, which is disastrous. To clarify this concept, what I mean is that we think about whether we would like to become doctors, lawyers, soldiers, musicians, teachers, etc., rather than think about whether we're good at negotiation, debate, painting, writing, etc. Barring few professions, which depend on extremely limited skill-sets—like modeling—we rarely think about all the intellectual tools required to succeed in a certain professional path, and this is where problems begin.

As children, and then again in our adolescence and adulthood, we're hell-bent on creating idealistic world-views of how we think life fits together in different scenarios—whether in a specific vocational field, geographic location, lifestyle, etc. But here's the truth—as long as we start off with the image in our head and then work backwards from it to make it come true, only 2 out of 7 of us will actually *like* what we find once we get there! Getting to a certain kind of life (within reason) is the easy part, but it's significantly harder to *guarantee* that you'll actually *like* that life. But, in working backwards from that image, we also create an image of our own personality as we believe it to be necessary to fit into that life. And then, after getting there, we feel deeply dissatisfied by it once we realize that—no matter how well we thought we could predict our feelings in that particular life—it *always* feels different from how we thought it would be!

So, the very first thing which you need to do if you truly wish to find your calling in life is to let go of this belief of absolute certainty which we tag along like a sack of moldy potatoes. Rather than helping us, or even making us more confident—which is why most people lug it around—it slows us down, and prevents us from discovering real joy and purpose, or from enjoying our life to the absolute fullest.

This may be quite a scary process, and is significantly more difficult than it may seem at first, but in order to progress along this path all you need to do is to accept that there may be things about yourself and your preferences in life which you may not have prioritized in a manner which would be more conducive to your joyful success in the world—rather than being dissuaded and deluded either by ourselves, our environment, or even just by money. Accepting this doesn't mean that your life will fall apart, or that you will suddenly cease to be good at things you're currently performing well in, but just that it will open you up to options which were left unconsidered, and which you may or may not then follow—depending on your own choice.

If you truly feel that you're losing your purpose in life—if you didn't, then you wouldn't be reading this book to begin with—then the very first thing you also need to let go off is the certainty that your current life works well for you. You may also believe that everything except "detail xyz" is perfect, and if that single element changed then everything else would be just hunky-dory. I'm sorry but that's not the way life works. It's rather like those children's block-matching games—you either fit well in your life, or you don't. If you only had trouble with one detail in your life, then your innate ability to compromise—which is rather large I'm afraid, as proven by the fact that your current life isn't the one you really wanted deep down but didn't change till now—would have allowed you to gloss right over it. Also, the choice of professional careers is often dictated by personality and dreams (and very rarely by skill-sets and dreams), so if you're possibly in the wrong career, then your true personality is yet to fully show itself.

In such times, it's rather tempting to make excuses and think that you over-reacted, or are having something of a mid-life crisis, but it's not like everyone has a mid-life crisis either. If you need to find your true purpose in life, or feel that you're in the wrong place, stop making excuses. Take a deep breath, and just admit to yourself that your life may need some significant changes if you wish to be happy. And why not? Everyone deserves to be happy, to be filled with the enthusiasm of their purpose in life—not only does that make people more joyous, but also more engaged and less apathetic towards their quality of life.

Also, it's rather important to point out that letting go of concrete certainty isn't the same as regret—the former is important, the latter is not. If there are elements which you treasure in your life, then the only thing you know for sure is that it's the path that you've conclusively taken—the choices you've made, etc.—that have allowed those elements to develop in you. Moreover, there's no way to know for sure that you would've been mentally and intellectually capable of following your path at any time before this one. So, no one's asking you to regret your past—quite the opposite in fact, since regret holds you back.

Now, only you can know for sure if you've successfully managed to dump this unhealthy certainty or not. If you have, then give yourself a hearty pat on the back since you just overcame an incredible obstacle. Only when you've dropped the delusion that your perspective of your "reality" (which, by its very nature, is a deeply subjective construct) is the most accurate one, your mind can successfully open up to let in new or previously hastily dismissed ideas.

Chapter 2: Discovering Yourself — the Paper "You"

While it may sound really clichéd, the next step is to figure out who you are at this point in your life. And this time, the idea is to do it right, so take out a pen and paper—it's time you met your proxy paper self.

Now, the idea of a proxy paper self isn't to create a 15-second elevator pitch-version of who you are—but rather to delve deep down and create a DNA blueprint of everything you know about yourself. This is also a time for deep introspection, and to figure out the aspects of your personality which have significantly changed since the last time you thought about yourself. If you're a teen though, you can skip that part—because the last time was half a minute ago when, with all the focused attention of a gnat, you took a break from reading to post a silly selfie of yourself.

Either way, in all seriousness, close yourself off in a quiet and comfortable space and create a relaxed environment for yourself. Once you've done that, grab the pen and paper—specifically, since the very act of putting pen to paper and shaping letters helps open up closed off thoughts as well—and start creating a cheat-sheet of yourself which includes all your pluses and minuses.

Within this list, first list all of your character attributes—short tempered, patient, analytical, impassioned, silver-tongued, puzzle-lover, philanthropic, organized, love traveling, etc. Be honest with yourself, and list all positive and negative attributes without negotiating with yourself or trying to be dishonest in order to paint yourself in a better light. The truer you are to yourself, and the more your real confessions here are at odds with how you thought of yourself up till this point, the better you would be able to understand the true depth of your discontent with your current life.

Once you've finished listing your attributes, make a check-mark next to the ones which you linked to your own behavior in a positive light before you sat down for this introspective exercise—the behavioral characteristics which you believe would lead you to success in any field. After this, list any and all skill-sets which you possess—carpentry, crafting, dancing, sailing, cooking, writing, wine-tasting, etc. Include any and all traits which require experience and skill to develop, and which you can perform at a beginner to expert level. Once you're done jotting them all down, mark "beginner", "intermediate", and "expert" next to each skill—and mark yourself with absolute honesty, but don't be unnecessarily harsh or unfairly critical. It's just as important to not undervalue yourself as it is to not overvalue yourself in such endeavors. If there are any particular guilty pleasures which add depth to your skills, like "informed knowledge of art movies in the 70s", and if you've enjoyed writing reviews about them in the past—add that information next to the relevant skill.

After these particular additions to the page, make check-marks next to the skills which give you absolute pleasure and which continue to excite you to this day. Keep in mind that these don't necessarily need to be the skills you've already mastered, but could also just be ones which you've developed to intermediate levels over time by investing your own private time into them. Regardless, the point here is to grant sorely-needed recognition to your true interests rather than the ones which may have ruled your life and professional choices up until this point. However, this doesn't mean that some of them don't overlap—if you were an English professor so far, with a penchant for script-writing, a sharp wit to boot, and a keen understanding of the interest points of people, you could be interested in advertising as a future option.

This exercise ignores questions such as degrees and qualifications for a specific reason—they may or may not have anything to do with fields in which you'd love to get involved. Involving them in the consideration defeats the purpose of this exercise, which aims at straightening out who you are outside the boundaries of your professional or academic path so far. If your favorite career would be the one you'd already set yourself to achieve, it would reflect in your choices above—regardless of whether or not your qualifications are considered.

Once you've finished all the steps, take a look at the completed blueprint of yourself—and try to gauge if the results surprise you, or whether you had already expected the final image to come out the way it did. If your evaluation turned out to be rather as you expected—kick yourself, because you just wasted your time when you knew the solution to your problem all along. Simply follow the path which you already knew you should have, and forge the career which you truly wanted to take up rather than the one you chose.

If your evaluation of yourself threw up a few surprises, particularly as to whether or not you realized which of your skills gave you most satisfaction and a sense of peace—then you have some deep introspection to get done with, before you can successfully craft ways in which you can assume your proper place in a world which would seem like your own, rather than one which you were forced into through erroneous choices or circumstances.

Chapter 3: Utilizing Enthusiasm, Not Logic

After having identified the skill-sets and traits on your list which you would enjoy the most as part of your vocation, as well as which would bring you success in any chosen field, the next step which you need to take is to figure out how to turn that into an actionable career plan. In this step, you need to check combinations of different skill-sets and determine the ones among them that could result in interesting and profitable vocations. However, make sure to stick to that specific order alone—first comes interest, and then the money. You don't want to start following the money, and make the same mistake you made the first time around.

In this part, you could mix skill-sets like cooking with attributes like your love of traveling to open up a food truck, or photography and hiking to become a nature and wildlife photographer, etc. The point is to identify as many of such combinations as you could in order to present yourself with viable job options. Don't get too hung up on the idea of logic or reason if you can't come up with options which are traditionally considered established professions either. It wasn't that long ago that the only food trucks would be ice-cream sellers, and today people have built an entire foodie sub-culture around gourmet or fast-food trucks, with loyal clientele that travel all over their city to get a taste of their culinary offerings. Being a professional reviewer didn't pay great either, till YouTube's partnership program came along and boosted the growth of content-driven entrepreneurial models like that of PewDiePie. The primary criteria here should always remain directions which inspire you, rather than one which forms the easiest source to money in your mind. However, if those two criteria lead you to the same conclusion, more power to you!

Once you've decided on a few plausible career paths, get down to research—and check if such professions already exist in your city, and whether or not they have established and thriving markets. If they already exist—which will always be the case, since there are very few jobs which haven't already been thought of by someone somewhere—get your hands on as much resource material as you can to gather more information on the realities of your chosen field. This means that, by the end of your research, you should have a decent idea of the demand for your "product" in your city, as well as a clear idea of scope for progress and development, and an identifiable starting point or platform which you could use to professionally launch yourself onto that path once you deem yourself ready. Your research should also uncover any and all improvement courses or classes which you could possibly take in order to increase the prospective market value of your offering—whatever that may be. If you've always worked in corporate environments, and wish to strike it on your own with this venture, you may also want to attend some business and entrepreneurship courses or seminars around you in order to get a better idea of what it's like to work for yourself.

Beside such mundane concerns, you should also have a clear idea in your head about any equipment which you may need in the course of pursuing your passion, as well as costs of the upgraded league of equipment you'd eventually like to acquire. If you're sufficiently driven about garnering an income through such means, it won't take you too long to start checking items off that list through your new earnings. Do not attempt to use savings to buy the best possible equipment for your new career plan right off the bat. Skills can only truly develop and improve in times when you're *lacking* things that you need. Such periods will force you to come up with creative solutions posed to problems which you may face.

Lastly, your research should also tell you who among the people in your personal or (current) professional networks may help provide more value to your business—either through business referrals, contacts who are in similar professions, or through directly teaching you something about it which you could not have learnt or understood by reading up about it on your own.

Chapter 4: Switching over to a Different Path

If you're already set on pre-determined paths, but don't like where you're heading, the question of how and when to switch over becomes rather crucial in its timing. The thought may give you some apprehensions or worries—but don't be concerned, we'll help you figure out the best way for you to get on the right track for your calling in life.

If you already have an established career, and have people depending on you to bring home the bacon, it may not be wise to make large-scale changes right away. You can create interesting professions out of your skill-sets, and try them out as side-streams for extra income at first. You could even try integrating them into your normal life, just to see how well you can perform at them. For example, if you're interested in landscape photography, you could try hiking up hills and mountains in your area to take interesting wide-shot or aerial-shots of your city, and then offering them to local publications for use in their material.

Once you've had a few photographs accepted by them, you could try approaching them for freelance work during your days off. In this manner, you can work on your skills and gauge your value in your chosen field. As I mentioned, interest should trump logic here—and the theories of business state that the more unusual your chosen market, the higher are your chances of successfully establishing yourself in a niche. So, don't worry about the traditional aspects of professional careers, and simply get to discovering jobs which would be interesting, exciting, and challenging for you to perform.

However, if you're a student then you're in a far more favorable position. In such a case, my advice to you will be to first check if you're truly serious about your new calling by attempting to dip your toe in it while continuing on your current path for a short time—no longer than a couple of months. This is going to be a difficult time for you since you're going to need to concentrate on your current studies harder than you have so far, as well as push to find more about your chosen "calling" which you determined through the paper proxy exercise.

The reason why I suggest trying harder in both fields is that, for some people, when their current chosen path starts throwing up difficulties they tend to balk and look for ways to get out rather than see them through. This creates an attitude of escapism for the rest of your life which, regardless of which career you follow, will always nip at your heels whenever you run into problems. So, instead of switching over right away, spend some time learning about the realities of your desired profession—for example, if you're studying to become a doctor, but want to go into advertising instead, check with resources to figure out the necessary qualifications for the field and whether or not you have the creative ability to do well there. Once you've ascertained that you can truly succeed there, stop wasting time and switch over to the necessary degree as fast as you can.

Now, from personal experience, this step is far harder than it sounds. There are many considerations which come up to hold people back from wanting to make this change—concerns over familial reactions if they were financing your current education, apprehensions about whether you should finish your current course and then switch fields, etc. Well, if you're very close to finishing your field—say, a few months—by all means, stay and finish it first. But if you're in your second year or so of your studies, then stop wasting time and money, and switch over to the necessary course for your chosen calling as soon as possible. Don't think of it as time and money wasted, because all of your past experiences have brought you to the realization of your true purpose. Soon you will be more successful in a field you happily chose rather than the field you just happened to get into.

Chapter 5: Distinguishing between Constructive Criticism & Naysayers

At this point in your shift to your chosen calling, you should recognize the fact that your confidence—regardless of how you externally project it to be—might be a little shaky. And that's understandable. After all, you'll have many doubts and apprehensions about whether or not you're doing the right thing, especially since you're switching your life in midstream.

In such times, you'll be surrounded by two kinds of people—those who just say nay, and those who wish to help you by offering constructive criticism. And it's absolutely vital that you maintain the analytical ability to distinguish between them before you allow their opinions to sway your mind.

Naysayers will have nothing more to offer you than pessimistic worries and concerns without offering any solutions for them. They will tell you that you're incapable of following such a path, or that the career in itself is unworthy or a joke—without giving you any detailed or logical explanations for their opinion beyond the straightforward impression that that's just how they *feel*. Ignore such people with all your might.

Not only are they bitter or obstructionist, in some cases they may plainly just not understand you and your priorities or may just be speaking from a place of their own vested fears. Such people raise apprehensions or doubts which have more to do with how they perceive their own professions or their own capabilities, than any tangible measure of intellectually supported arguments.

On the other hand, people with constructive criticism will have a rather different approach—whether or not they agree with your choices. Such people, even if they offer pessimistic views or concerns about your decision, will also offer ways for you to better understand your chosen path, or get a measure of your relevant skills for it, or even ways to improve yourself if they feel you may be lacking something important which is required for success in your field. While these people may or may not whole-heartedly support your decision, they will still offer ways for you to improve upon your foundation and chances of success—rather than just telling you that it won't work and leaving it at that. Even if they have serious doubts about this endeavor, they will always supplement their argument with well-reasoned points, and then attempt to help you overcome the problems they foresee so that you can achieve your goals.

Understanding the difference between these two is crucial to build a support system which you can depend on—particularly since you'll have doubts and fears of your own. People in your shoes, when faced with such people, behave in a few predictable ways—either by letting the naysayers erode their confidence and change their minds about a decision which does benefit them immensely when taken up again in the future, or by lashing out against those who offer constructive criticism since they feel that they have no one's support and they fail to distinguish that this group (regardless of their personal opinion on the matter) *is* trying to help them solidify their chances of success in their new path. The first reaction simply prolongs an anguish which could have ended right then, and stops you from making a decision which would do you a world of good and help you establish a life which you enjoy and cherish. The second one stops you from benefitting from the experience and wisdom of others who are trying to help you improve and develop for success.

Regardless of whether or not someone *agrees* with you isn't a mark of whether or not they *support* you—don't ever confuse those two aspects when determining a support system. The job of a good support system *is* to question you in order to understand your motives better, and you should have enough confidence in yourself to give a confident explanation and strong answer.

However, once they've questioned you, a support system will offer improvements, advice, and wisdom which would help you plan your switch better or even aid you in navigating your new path with more ease— whether or not they agree. And the primary reason why I keep stressing upon "whether or not they agree" is that, regardless of which direction your career may take you, someone who cares for you and wishes to support you so that you can realize your full potential would never want you to stagnate in a profession that made you miserable. They would be glad that you've found a direction in life which lights the fires of passion in your life—even if they didn't quite understand it.

Always maintain a cool head that would allow you to distinguish between these two kinds of people. Use a level head rather than emotions to create a support system that wants the best for you, rather than one which needlessly obstructs you—and you will achieve heights in your calling which you could have never imagined otherwise.

Conclusion

Steve Jobs would have made an awful Jay Leno, and an even worse Winston Churchill. People have long believed that, regardless of where you work, there are a few directions in *everyone's* lives where they could truly climb to the top and out-shine all others—and this belief makes absolute sense. The personality and skill-sets of each individual always combine in ways which would make them absolutely perfect for one or two career paths—as long as they can determine those professions. If someone is intelligent enough, they can offset their disadvantages in any profession and do reasonably well enough—and yet, they could have ruled the roost had they just taken time to figure out their calling.

Whether you're a student, or you're already working, moments that make you re-think your direction in life are joyous occasions which don't grace everyone. They essentially mean that you're capable of far higher levels of success than you'd envisioned so far, so don't waste them.

Instead of letting doubts and apprehensions bog you down—which would ultimately end up with you simply throwing it all away and sticking to your current path—take the process step by step. Don't let yourself get overwhelmed by side-considerations, and instead, try to approach each problem that you foresee as an intellectual exercise. Apart from the solutions which you come up with yourself, consult your support system for their advice and wisdom as well—even if you think you know better than they do. Don't forget to distinguish between the naysayers and genuine supporters within your advisors, and tweak your support structures in a way that minimizes your intellectual dependence and interaction with those who won't encourage or boost you.

Finding your calling in life is easy—as long as you have the guts to be honest with yourself, and perform the paper proxy exercise with absolute integrity. Switching to a new life, and turning it into a successful career path, isn't the hard part either. The most difficult segment to negotiate in this entire process is the state of limbo in the middle—when you've recognized the direction you want to head in, and are attempting to break across. The only things that make this crossing treacherous are the alligators of self-doubt and apprehension lurking under the water. Acknowledge them, since you need to see them to avoid them, but don't let yourself get dragged down by them. You will be your own worst enemy at this point, and as long as you remain confident in your analysis and evaluation, you'll make it across without a hitch.

Go, conquer your fears and grab success by the horns.

Finally, I'd like to thank you for purchasing this book! If you enjoyed it or found it helpful, I'd greatly appreciate it if you'd take a moment to leave a review on Amazon. Thank you!

Made in the USA
San Bernardino, CA
29 May 2017